DOWN IN THE DUGOUTS

A Collection of Poems by

William A. Roberts

A.H. STOCKWELL
PUBLISHERS SINCE 1898

Published in 2023 by
William A. Roberts
East Malling, Kent
in association with
Arthur H Stockwell Ltd
West Wing Studios
Unit 166, The Mall
Luton, Bedfordshire
ahstockwell.co.uk

British Library Cataloguing-in-Publication Data
A catalogue record for this book is
available from the British Library.

The views and opinions expressed herein belong to the author and do not necessarily reflect those of AH Stockwell

Contents

Contents (cont.)

Down in the Dugouts

Socks, Pants and Vest

Raising the standard, that's the job of the wife,
Making me look sharp and dandy like a well-honed knife.
She always makes me conscious of my dress
And every morning puts out my clean socks, pants and vest.

But she says she's fighting a losing battle,
That I make something inside her really rattle.
You see I don't always bother with my sense of dress
And don't always change my socks, pants and vest.

The Ovens are Hot

Load them up and ship them out,
Don't worry about their screams and shouts.
The ovens are hot, the chambers cold,
Watch the poor wretches cling and hold
Onto each other, child and mother.
The gas is ready at the flick of a switch,
Then watch them panic, die and twitch.

Bath Night

Fires burning brightly, there's chestnuts in the hearth,
Kids are dripping wet, they've just got out of the bath,
Wrapped in towels they sit beside the fire,
Watching the flames flicker through the wire guard.
Blowing on their chestnuts they eat them by the score,
Shucks are in the bowl and all across the floor.

And as the last nut disappears into a hungry mouth
All the kids get their night clothes on and head on south,
Up the stairs and into bed
Dreaming sweet dreams that dance in their heads.

Down in the Dugouts

Down in the dugouts men cower in fear,
Rifles and mortars held as near as a lover.
Sweat beads the brow, anytime now
And it's over the top, time ticks away ever so slowly.
Enemy awaits, machine guns open wide spewing death,
Taking the breath away for the last time.

The Lost Freedom

Once I was free, free as a bird, free as the wind.
I had nothing or nobody to hold me down,
I would walk tall and proud, head held high,
Sun shining in the sky every day, but then I met you,
Fell in love, fell into your web of deceit,
Told me you would never change me; that was five years ago.
Now my head hangs low and there's a stoop in my walk.

Bravery by the Sea

I was brave down by the sea, it happened so fast.
One minute I was fully clothed and walking in the sand,
Holding the hand of my true love, the next
I was overcome with emotion.
The sun was out, smiling it seemed, gulls
flew around screaming for titbits.
I had this overwhelming need to take my shoes and socks off,
Roll up my trouser legs and have a paddle – so I did.

Blood-Red Hands

I wash my hands a dozen times a day,
But still I cannot wash the blood away,
Blood that had once coursed through living men,
Now damp and lifeless as the ink from this pen.

The stench and stain will never dry,
Each night alone I lie and cry.
Many men have died in the name of war,
Now only the dead walk across my bedroom floor.

Faces smashed, loss of limb,
Eyes once alive and smiling, now dark and dim,
Talking with mouths that speak no words,
Huddled like cattle in monstrous herds,

All crammed in my bedroom every night,
Pointing at my blood-red hands in the pale moon light.

The Phone

When you put the phone down sometimes there's a dialling tone,
Which could mean that someone else is on the phone.
You're more than likely talking to someone new,
I hope this is the case because I need to talk to you.

But the real reason is you forgot to replace the handset
And I'll be calling you for days… just you bet.
So put the handset down gently and we can start anew,
You talking to me and me talking to you.

But What of the Mothers?

I can see all the suffering and decay
On this our longest day.
The beaches are full of bullet-ridden men,
As I put it down on paper with my artful pen.

Barbed wire is strewn across the sand
And blood soaks into the foreign land.
Our men are dying, never more to be seen,
Just so that the world is sterile and clean

But what of the mothers who wait at home
And lovers of loved ones waiting alone?
What of them, what can we do?
Never forget … that's what we should do,
Never forget the suffering and pain
And hope with all our heart that there's no more war again.

School

To write and speak better there is but one simple rule
And that is that every day you should go to school,
To learn about yesterdays and of days to come,
Try not to be naughty or they'll cane your bum.

School can be a rough old place where bullies reign supreme,
Or it can be a place of love where you'll find the girl of your dreams,
But all said and done when the day is through,
You will have the happy knowledge of knowing something new.

A Length of Rope

You've drunk your tea, now there's things to do,
Like ironing, sewing and polishing too,
Hoovering, bedmaking then cooking tea,
No time to waste, he'll be home you see.

Then it's TV for an hour, maybe a little bit more,
Then the same old things like so many times before,
Beer and a fondle, bed and a grope,
God, I'd give my right arm for a length of rope.

Broken Spell

Once I was in love. I had everything, or so I thought.
House, car, wife and children – even a job,
But then reality took over,
Illness crept in … and the spell was broken.

You're a Stain

You're a stain in my life, an open sore,
One that's forever weeping, deep down to my core,
Pus and blood seeping free, go… go… get away from me.
I don't want your begging or any of your pleading, just let me be,
While I'm grieving just go, leave me alone… I've had enough of you.

The Taste of a Gun

I look across the trenches to where the enemy lie
And know in my heart that today I will die.
The killing fields of France are strewn with the dead and dying,
I cover my ears to the screams and the crying.
Death is all around me, I have nothing to gain.
Tasting the cool barrel of my gun, I send a bullet though my brain.

Poverty

Where you find poverty you usually find war,
Be it a nation against nation or your neighbour next door.
Poverty is the scourge amongst all mankind,
But when it is far away we tend to go blind.

We tend not to think of all those poor souls,
Thin as rakes and meagre rice in bowls.
We sit at home, our bellies full
And we are deaf to the call.
Children starve and children die,
It's enough to make a grown man cry.

If only he could.

Sea Levels

Sea levels are rising, land's slipping away.
Fishes don't mind, they love it this way,
Birds of the air don't seem to care,
Four-footed animals who live on the land,
Scientists have found they're having a breakdown.
What of man, do we worry?... no no,
Too much of a hurry for the 59 bus.

Storm

There's a storm brewing, clouds big black boiling angry,
So angry, threatening to tear the sky apart.
Lightning, brilliant silver, zigzagging downwards downwards,
Punching the earth in such a frenzy… just the way I feel.

Turmoil

The world's in turmoil, we're running amok, beatings, rapes killings etc,
Can nothing stop us? No… no… maybe it's time to wake the dead.
Good idea: cry out as one, "Wake the dead… Wake the dead…"
Sod it – let 'em sleep.

A Good Fight

Watched boxing last night, good fight. "Punch him in the eye," I cried,
And those inside ducked and dived for cover, except my mother,
who punched *me* in the eye for messing up
my sister's wedding reception.

Food

I'm in disbelief, a state of shock,
My whole world has been rocked
By what I see and hear, fear has gripped the planet,
From the Himalayas with llamas and Africa's Savanna,
Monkeys wearing brightly coloured bandanas,
A flask of tea (two sugars and a little milk if you please),
Sitting under trees carefully, so very carefully
Eating what is not allowed.
The government is here shouting "Don't eat this, don't eat that,"
And the monkeys who are watching and listening
Whispered "WHAT A LOAD OF CRAP."

The Face of God

And so the Lord God called man unto him
And man knelt face-down in the dirt and awaited God's words.
And the Lord God said,
"I am very old, my children, 'tis time for me to die."
And man, so shocked at the news and fearful,
Looked up and saw the face of God and it was all too much for man,
And he screamed and screamed and screamed.

Being Mum

I don't give a toss, you still have to wash
Because I say so. Now go upstairs to the bathroom,
Don't forget behind your ears, now come on, lovely, dry those tears,
It won't take long, you can even sing a song while you wash.
You're all smelly and there'll be no telly
Until you've done as you're told.
Yes I know I'm old fashioned, but I'm still your mother.

Mother Nature

Things have changed, nothing's the same any more,
The world is getting faster and fuller and
now there's a hole in the ozone,
And to top it all the ice-caps are melting.
Global warming is what the boffins say …
I say it's madness and we should all take care,
Or Mother Nature will get angry and send us to bed hungry.

Abattoir

Feel the cold, so cold, and you can smell the fear from the animals.
The smell of blood hangs heavy in the air,
While death is the only escape for those poor wretches,
Hung up and throats cut,
They run their own life away, such a slow death
And all the while man is getting plumper, fatter,
He begins to look good... tasty in fact.

Tipsy Fly

Have you ever watched a spider when it has caught its prey?
It races down upon it in a horrifying way.
Two huge fangs lunge into soft flesh
And then cocooned for later in a silken mesh.
Still alive and frightened, the fly lies helpless in its fear.
I bet the little bleeder wishes now it had left well alone my beer.

I've Mislaid the Wife

4.30am in the morning and what am I doing here?
There's no more Tegretol to take and I haven't got a beer.
My brain is on overload, my mind's about to explode,
And looking into bloodshot eyes, my contours begin to erode.
I have shaking hands and a hangover from the night before,
And I can't find the wife anywhere after the slamming of the door.

Pain

Take this heart and feel my pain over and over again,
Feel it beating brokenly like the tears that I cry.
No blue sky or bright warm summer sun,
Just the smoking of your hand gun.

Heaven

I'm in heaven looking down at a bright green world,
With crystal blue seas, animals which no longer tear each other apart.
Peace cloaks the earth and celebrates each new birth,
Playing and jumping and just being happy and then
And then man came along, what more can I say?

War

Trench warfare is the worst where shells explode and bodies burst,
Where hand-to-hand fighting is commonplace,
always aiming at your opponent's face.
Smash his skull, rip out his guts, use knives, spades or rifle butts,
Use anything you can just so that you live
One more day inside of you... more killing to give.

Ship on Fire

There's a ship on fire out at sea, plumes of
black smoke can be seen easily.
Two lifeboats tearing through the waves – will they get there?
I don't think so… there are quite a few people standing alone,
Small groups just looking out to sea, the big yellow sun is watching,
Golden sand hot underfoot, there's a lot of murmuring.
People seem to be holding their breath.
Looking down I spy a small child, little yellow beach bucket in hand,
Knee deep in the sea I watch… no one else seems to notice but I do.
He fills his little bucket with water and throws
it towards the stricken ship.
God love innocents.

Youth of Today

Phone call or colour blind, pork rind and
beans, gangster moll and screams,
Baby dreams and cold streams of water, they caught her,
Stripped her, beat her and raped her, left her
for dead, hid her body in a shed.
Wooden floor stained red, the gangster in all of
this kissed his girl and went to bed.
He was only fourteen and had to be in by nine.

Family Troubles

Please don't touch me, leave me alone,
I'm just sitting her quietly waiting for the phone.
She could be ringing anytime soon,
Please step back give me some room.
Yes… it *is* a body that I am sitting on.
I've been here for a while, it's so long she started to stiffen,
Her blood to congeal. I know she will phone me, it's a matter of time,
I'm her husband and will be for all time.

A Lovely Day to Die

It's a lovely day to die,
Not a cloud in the sky.
A man could ask for nothing more…
Except an end to this infernal war.

Courting Death

I took a walk down the winding lane, all leafy in the pouring rain.
I was going to the Frog Pond, where me and my girl were very fond,
Sitting on the edge where there's a ledge and holding each other tight
Through the night, cuddles and kisses. She's another man's missus,
But I don't care. I hoped he'd share this beautiful woman with me.
The answer to this is no, he proved this when he showed up at the pond.
He found us together, now we will be forever together, united as one,
Bloated and lifeless under the water.

Poor Little Orange

From where I am sitting I can see an orange in its bowl.
It truly breaks my heart, it looks such a lonely soul,
Round and orange and as sad as can be.
Perhaps it's a little frightened that it'll be eaten by me,
But it must not fear me, I'm not the one with the knife
That's held in the delicate hand of my sweet darling wife.

Sentry Duty

He passed so close by me with his heavy load,
The holes in his hands and feet through the dimness glowed.
"Halt who goes there?" I called into the night.
He turned to face me, his thorns were bright.
I could see by the light his face was weary
And when I looked into his eyes...
I saw that they were teary.

No One's Laughing

The sky is getting cloudy and there's trouble on the way.
It has nothing to do with the weather… war has broken out today.
Everyone's in a panic but there's nowhere left to run,
In the beginning everyone thought it would be oh so fun,
But now in the cold grey light of day, everyone can see
The full horror of war… and it's not so funny.

You Can't Imagine

You cannot imagine unless you had been there,
The smell of rotting corpses all due to warfare.
Skeletal forms crushed and broken,
Mouths agape… words unspoken.

You cannot imagine unless you had been there,
The smell of mustard gas that would fill the air,
Shells that would explode and tear you apart,
Machine guns rattling death and then it would start.

Over the top and into hell,
You just can't imagine the noise and the smell.

Sunday Morning Bliss

Sunday morning 5am and the streets are deserted;
Even the cars are taking a well-deserved rest.
No chirping of bird, no barking of dog,
No mother screaming at her little angels.
All is quiet, even the wife's asleep.
It's bliss.

Shells

Have you ever heard a horse scream as it's thrown into the air?
It doesn't bother shells, they just don't care.
Animals, men, machinery too, shells explode and rip in two,
Heads ripped off so there's no more charm,
And if you're very lucky you'll lose only an arm.
Limbs lie about with nothing much to do,
Pointing every which way accusing you.
You can hear them coming and you duck so low,
Heart pounding so hard you think it will blow,
And then there is silence and again you live,
Listening to the screams of the dying… they have no more to give.

Justification

Does being in the army justify killing?
You have to be willing and hungry to take a man's life,
Bullet or knife up close, look into his eyes,
See the fear, hear the tormented cry of a lost soul.
Is *this* what you want?

My Dislikes

I don't like swearing nor do I like to cuss,
Nor do I like to run for the number 9 bus.
I don't like puddles after the rain,
I don't like holidays especially to Spain.
I'd rather have a steam than electric trains,
And with this gun I'm going to blow out my brains.
Just after I kill you, my love…

And the Lord God Spoke

And the Lord God spoke unto man saying this earth is mine creation,
Thou art mine creation, I have made thee in mine own image,
And I have charged thee to be guardian over all
The earth and its creatures, take care now.

But man poisoned the earth and killed every living thing,
And the Lord God saw this and was angry with man.
He sent floods and thunder and lightning down upon the earth,

And man was afraid, but he turned back to the Lord God,
And prayed and begged for mercy, but the
Lord God was deaf to his cries,
And so man was smote from the earth that
the Lord God had given to him.

Dark Days

There's no escape, nowhere to turn, just like fire
My heart it burns, fear it grips me to the point of death.
I walk this world deaf to any sound around me, my eyes are blind.
No kind of light, not even the brightest of bright, penetrates through.
My tongue is silent, never more to speak,
Awash with tears I cry silently to myself,
Lips forming the words "I LOVE YOU."

I Can Fly

There's quite a crowd down there looking up at me.
I'm on top of the multi-storey carpark wall looking down.
It's a long way down there.
I've been reading and watching those Superman films and comics.
I know I can do it, fly that is,
Arms outstretched, look up, smile, lean forwards and FREE FALL…

Country Walk

Every day I walk a mile through fields over stiles,
Little lambs frolicking, having fun, bleating,
Bleating in the warmth of the sun,
Jacket off and over my shoulder,
Get to the end of the field one mile older.

Dreaming

When I rolled over I broke my shoulder,
And the algae in the lake looked green,
Unseen from afar in a car,
And fishes were happily swimming about, especially the trout,
And the cat waited patiently, waited and waited,
And is still waiting there now…

An Unkind Act

After midnight, under a cloak of darkness,
I crept up to his house and kicked his dog.
That's why the police took me… animal cruelty.

Nothing Like a Good Hanging

Be good, be kind, don't leave anyone behind.
Pig rind and apple sauce, very tasty dish,
Of course, little children, strawberry jelly and cream,
Night terrors and screams not just dreams,
New ropes hanging from wooden rafters,
Bodies hanging, people's laughter, think it fun
To watch them die twitching and shaking,
Eyes bulging out from their heads.
A few more drinks and then off home
To a nice warm bed,
Better than going to the cinema… much better.

Gloomy Surroundings

I put the curtains up and pulled them to,
Lovely in length, no light shining through,
Only one wooden chair in the middle of the room.
No light bulbs, no candles in this perpetual gloom.
Floor is a mess, warped and wooden boards,
So many ants about, quite a show (hate them really).
They bite me, don't you know, nasty little buggers.

If Only

I'd like to paint the morning sky reds and yellows, orange and blue.
If I could capture this beauty on canvas I would have it framed
And give it to you, if I could walk a million miles
I would do this willingly just to see you smile,
If I could hold you one last time, but alas I cannot,
Because you're no longer mine.

Crash

All of my thoughts, all of my feelings,
All those spiders on the ceiling.
Car crashes outside the house,
Hide inside, quiet as a mouse.
Ambulance comes and so do the police,
Drunk driver they do not release.
Handcuffed and put in to the back of the van.
Go to bed, head reeling,
Bloody spiders still on the ceiling.

Hallucinating

I'm sure you know what I am doing,
Running around the house,
Shooing all the little elves and trolls alike,
Sister Sara and brother Mike.
I've chased the little sods all over the place.
You can't see them, it shows on your face.
I've run myself ragged and now I want my bed,
Don't worry about feeding me, I've already been fed.
I put my hand in the glass bowl and ate all the goldfish.

Isolationist

I could quite easily live on my own,
No TV, computer or phone (mobile or otherwise),
No one tell me what I can and can't do.
I hit the dog with a shoe.
Alone in my flat to the mirror I go,
Smiling at me, smiling back.
All goes dim – heart attack.

Unwelcome Visitor

Just a note to say I won't be home any more.
I've been arrested for what I've done.
Before on the farm where I lived,
The farmer would come to me at night.
I was petrified, he was such a formidable sight,
Smashed out of his head on a bottle of rye,
Big red nose and bloodshot eyes,
Beat beat beat me with the buckle of his belt.
When he left I was covered in welts,
Big red and angry ones.
I couldn't get to sleep in my bed.

Searching

For millennia they searched for the Holy Grail to no avail,
And the bride was covered by a veil of lace over her face,
Shy and sweet dainty hands and feet,
And the churches rushed headlong into chaos.

Love Is Forever

Turn back time to a place when things were fine,
And we loved and laughed so young and in love,
Hand in hand, my little dove,
We would talk for hours,
I'd buy you chocolates and flowers,
And you would love me again, but now so many years later
We have grown so very old – the spark's still there,
Our love's not cold – even now I love to hold you,
Tight in my arms as we sleep at night.
I love you, my darling wife.

The Man I Met

I passed a man in the street,
Had holes in his hands and holes in his feet,
His hair was unkempt and so was his beard,
He wore a robe but didn't look weird.
Upon his head was a thorny crown,
And he seemed quite happy to walk around town.

Watching You Eat

Anyone would think that you were half-starved
That way you pile it in, fork after fork.
You remind me of an open-cast mine.

Mum

Mum ain't well I can tell.
She made herself comfy on the settee,
Closing her eyes, breathing slowly, rhythmically.
Ain't no way she's going to the shop,
I was looking forward to a nice pork chop,
But buttered bread that's what it will be,
A few slices for you and a few slices for me.

Lost Love

I reach out with my hand and gently, tenderly touch your lips,
So soft warm and inviting, I yearn to kiss them to kiss you.
I open my eyes, my heart jumps, I look for you…

Afternoon Tea

Apple pie and custard and a creamy tea,
You made these especially for me,
Sitting smiling sweetly, love in your eyes.
No not for me, you want to cut all ties,
Another man is waiting patiently outside.
You kiss my cheek tenderly, we say our goodbyes,
Oh yes thank you, my darling, for my apple pie.

Coping With Loss

I watch you watching children as they run and laugh and play,
And I feel your loss.
I move closer to you and put my arm around you,
I feel you tighten slightly, momentarily,
Then you relax and allow yourself to be led gently away.

Poised

I'm poised ready, but nothing emerges.
I hold my pen over the paper as though I were
some native waiting in the shadows,
Spear in hand, sweat beading his brow, waiting
to strike at some unsuspecting fish.

Third World War

Fingers blistered and swollen from being in the scalding sea,
Wind blowing the skin from the army,
Sun melting and bubbling in the afternoon sky,
Mushrooms were growing much too high

Who Knows You?

No one knows you, just as a leaf blows away
with the coming Autumn winds,
To be blown away into obscurity and beyond.

Obscure

Obscuring the darkness of your voice I find myself alone…
Too afraid to call your name, I reach out with ghostly hands,
But I cannot find you.

My Daddy

Daddy took me to the seaside, said he'd teach me to swim,
I looked at the great expanse of water and just could not go in.
At first he was a patient man, coaxing me with all manner of things,
But I could not be bought and to his hand I did cling.

I heard his voice changing as his patience wore thin.
Picking me up above his head, he threw me all the way in.
I felt the cold water cover me and I thought I would drown,
But then I heard a familiar sound.

"Swim, you bugger, swim." It was my daddy encouraging me,
As I splashed and gulped water from the sea,
Then two large hands reached out and plucked me from my fate,
Lifting me high in the air before it was too late.

"Don't tell mummy, will you, and I'll buy you a sweet."
But I just dropped down to the sand and clung to his feet.

After the Row

After the row while the air was still blue,
I took a walk to get away from you,
Out of the door and onto the street,
Echoes rebounding from angry feet.

The pavement was damp, there was dew on the grass,
I had to walk till my anger had passed,
Around the block and through the wood,
The cold dark night air felt so good.

Soon the anger had begun to wane,
And I thought of you and our home again.
Exhausted and damp I walked through the door,
Kissed you tenderly as though we were lovers once more.

You responded to my kiss and then began to cry,
And I kept on kissing you till your tears were all dry.

My Companion

I am not alone out in my fox-hole,
Death is at my side as I dig like a mole.
It's hard to dig on your belly but I'm an old hand now,
And death has appeared beside me, from where I know not how.
He doesn't help, he just sits and stares.
His eyes are as bright as the enemies' flares.

Joints of Meat

Leather boots and trenchcoats marching mile after mile,
So many weary faces hardly raise a smile.
This is it, lads, this is what it's all about,
Back home they're still recruiting, join the final bout.

Reality is a lot different though – mud, dirt and disease,
Bellies always hungry and bodies full of fleas,
Then comes the fighting, brutal and to the point,
Bodies lay crushed and broken like so many butchers' joints.

Stolen Bikes

There seems to be too many pushbikes that are being stolen,
How can we keep our kids on the move and rolling?
They've been nicked from out of sheds and outside of shops too,
I do hope it isn't one of you.
No of course not, silly me,
You're as good as good can be.

Put your Hands Together

Put your hands together and give me a round of applause,
'Cause the lady next door has just changed her drawers.
I'm not joking or telling a lie,
I can see her old ones hanging on the line with me own eye.
Sort of pink purply thongs they're called.
She's a smashing lass, though she's a little bald,
Shaves her head, so I'm led to believe,
Looks like a tree in winter without its leaves.

Together Again

A single tear blooms and pushes itself out from tired eyes.
You have been gone for too long now,
Now it's time we should be together again.
I hold your picture, now beginning to fade,
But the eyes so bright even after all this time.
The gas hisses from the fire but no flame tonight,
The smell isn't too bad and now I feel drowsy, sleepy.
You picture falls from my hand.

Judgement Day

And judgement day came and lightning ripped the skies apart,
Seas broke through their defences and crashed ashore,
Trees were uprooted by the winds and were hurled like javelins,
Mountains crumbled and man…
Man cried out for mercy but found none.

Carried Away

Blacker than night, a frozen heart,
Bodies being loaded onto a cart,
Calling for the dead carried outside.
Families and friends break down and cry,
The sun will no longer warm the day.
Stench of the dead, bloated and grey,
Look out the window, nothing to say.
Bowing my head, I fold my hands and pray.

Death Comes to Us All

Death comes to us all and as the breath finally leaves
us we slowly stiffen as rigor mortis sets in,
Like winter slowly stretching out across the land,
freezing everything momentarily in time.

Look at Her

Look at her asleep, curled into a ball,
Foetus position, her breathing rhythmical,
Soft, almost a whisper that is carried off by the wind.

Passing

I walked into the sea slowly, slowly till it covered me. It seemed
to caress me tenderly as if saying 'I will hold you night and
day, don't worry about your true love, she's gone away.
I'm here every day, every night – come let me hold you, come
into my embrace, come let me kiss away the tears that you cry.
Trust me on this – let yourself go, let me rock you to and
fro. Sleep in my arms, I will hush you to sleep.
I will never let you go, no more pain, no
more tears falling like winter rain.
So sleep, my angel sleep, sleep, sleep my darling.'

Gran

She sleeps upright in her favourite chair,
Head slightly drooped, mouth open as if to say something,
Anything that will stop her looking almost comical.

My Father

Memories of my father – oil, dirt, hands, belt,
Beatings… beatings… beatings…

The Riot

The sun was finally setting over the rooftops,
Rioting was now widespread but still contained by the cops,
Some had set cars alight and were throwing rocks,
And some of them had broken windows and had started looting shops.

Shields and batons were in use as missiles flew through the air,
The police had it all under control and didn't really care,
Rushing into the rioting crowd, batons whistle and sing,
The old and frightened stayed indoors and didn't say a thing.

After a nighttime of madness the crowds began to disperse,
Ambulances were full to the brim (but not the local hearse).
Many had been wounded that night, blood ran in the street,
Car fires had been put out, but you could still feel the heat.

All is now quiet in the street, stones and broken bottles lie everywhere,
It looks like the aftermath of a war, total devastation and bare.
The streets belong to the police now, I can see them out in force,
Where would we be without them?… it would be anarchy, of course.

A Beautiful Dream

I've walked the road to nowhere without a single care,
Heavy boots and rucksack, I made my way there.
Darkness was complete, void of any sound,
Just my laboured breathing and my feet pounding on the ground.
Onward… onward… onward all through the night,
And then in the distance day awakening, slowly rising,
What a beautiful sight, sitting on a grassy
mound looking towards the east.
Orange sun stretching over the horizon's crest.
Then… then I awake and find myself in bed.
Yawning and stretching, I scratch my sleepy head,
And smile a sleepy smile… what a lovely dream.

On the Beach

One sunny day I was far away, sitting on golden sand, ice in hand,
When out of the sand a small crab spied me,
pincers clacking nosily, nervously.
Ever so slowly he made his way over to me,
I smiled friendly towards him, he was still a little shy,
When suddenly out of the sky a big old seagull swooped down
And grabbed the little crab who made no sound, shock and disappear,
As he was taken into the air. Shrugging my shoulders, did I care?
No, I didn't. I still have my ice cream, so there…

Who's in Charge?

The world is in turmoil – chaotic events,
massive wildfires around the globe,
Floods of biblical proportions springing up all over the place,
Little children starving and frightened, nowhere to turn,
Women and girls beaten and raped,
Those in charge of the earth don't seem to care,
But I do… and it breaks my heart.

Also from William Roberts

I Saw the Moon Wink

& Other Poems

William A. Roberts

Milton Keynes UK
Ingram Content Group UK Ltd.
UKHW011819131023
430526UK00001B/76